July 24, 2009

Dearest Anne,

Thank you so very much for your loving support and encouragement. Your forward to this book is beautifully written. Please accept my heartfelt thanks! Let's keep in touch.

In Light and Love,

Deb

BELLOWED WHISPERS

Journeying Back to Who You Are

Debra J. Suchy

iUniverse, Inc.
New York Bloomington

Bellowed Whispers
Journeying Back to Who You Are

The information, ideas, and suggestions in this book are not intended as a substitute for professional advice specific to individual need. If you have physical or mental health concerns, please consult your personal physician or mental health practitioner. Neither the author nor the publisher shall be liable or responsible for any loss or damage allegedly arising as a consequence of your use or application of any information or suggestions in this book.

iUniverse books may be ordered through booksellers or by contacting:

iUniverse
1663 Liberty Drive
Bloomington, IN 47403
www.iuniverse.com
1-800-Authors (1-800-288-4677)

Because of the dynamic nature of the Internet, any Web addresses or links contained in this book may have changed since publication and may no longer be valid. The views expressed in this work are solely those of the author and do not necessarily reflect the views of the publisher, and the publisher hereby disclaims any responsibility for them.

ISBN: 978-1-4401-5111-8 (pbk)
ISBN: 978-1-4401-5112-5 (cloth)
ISBN: 978-1-4401-5113-2 (ebook)

Cover art and drawings created by Graham N. Currie.

Printed in the United States of America

iUniverse rev. date: 6/24/09

I dedicate my life's work and this book to my husband Craig,
Who loves me in every way;
And to my children, Madison and Aaron, who love me anyway.

MY SCRIPT, MY LIFE

Through my healing, learning, writing, and teachings, I inspire individuals to nurture their own spirituality. I create literature and nonfiction to stimulate thought and facilitate growth. I meaningfully interact with individuals and groups. I integrate my knowing into my daily living and carry out my life's work without ego. This work that I do is in our Creator's love and in the pursuit of the highest good for all. I am present in each moment and experience a healthy balance between work and play. I set and maintain healthy boundaries, personally and professionally. I have the serenity to accept the things I cannot change, the courage to change the things I can, and the wisdom to know the difference. I have the time and energy to do Reiki, meditate, exercise, and eat healthy foods every day, and I do so. I willingly clear stuck energy. I think and speak in kindness and in love, without judgment. I feel loved. I feel safe. I live joyfully and with financial abundance. I live with purpose on this planet, knowing I play my part in bringing hope and peace to others. I am forever grateful for my role as a woman on this planet, as it is only as a woman that I can be a mother, a wife, a daughter, a sister, and an aunt. I remain forever thankful for my husband, our children, and this life we share. This labor of love is my expression of thanks to our Creator and to Mother Earth for the ecstasy I know through our connectedness, nourishes my soul.

═ Contents ═

Acknowledgments xi

Foreword By Dr. Anne Marie Evers.................................. xiii

Introduction... xvii

Chapter 1.   The Magic of Rocks and Crystals.................1
    Magic Stones.. 1
    Rocks and Crystals 3

Chapter 2.   Laying on of Hands for Healing.................13
    Mom, Come Do Your Voodoo Thing............................13
    Reiki...16

Chapter 3.   Animal Totems...23
    Namaste, Baby Moose..23
    Moose Medicine 26

Chapter 4.   Angels among Us......................................31
    My Angel, My Teacher..31
    Angels 33

Chapter 5.   Healing Through Past Lives.........................41
    Anna's Story..41
    Past-Life Regression 43

Chapter 6.   Traveling through Time and Space............49
    Crossing Over...49
    Spirits on the Move...51

Chapter 7.   Dolphins 55

    My Dolphin Odyssey 55

    Swimming with Dolphins 61

Chapter 8.   Making Your Dreams Take Flight 67

    A Mother's Wish 67

    Creating What You Desire 71

Conclusion 75

Recommended Reading 77

= Acknowledgments =

I am profoundly grateful to Spirit and to each of the beings of light from other realms who support me in my journey. Thank you, Grandma Jean, Uncle Ticky, and David for finding your way back to me from the other side. Thank you also to Mother Earth, who in all her wisdom teaches me and guides me.

I am eternally grateful to my husband of twenty-seven years for loving me, as we all deserve to be loved, and for bringing serenity into my life. Craig, you are my precious "six of diamonds," and I am so very, very grateful. Thank you to my greatest teacher, Aaron. Thank you to my most joyful playmate, Madison. Thank you also to my wonderful parents, Audrey and Gordon Connery, for loving me so deeply and for supporting me, no matter what. Thank you to my in-laws, Tom and Betty Suchy for loving me as I am.

Thank you to all my teachers along the way and to all the authors I have quoted in this book. Thank you also to Deepak Chopra and Wayne Dyer, who are not mentioned specifically but whose work has inspired me to be more of who I really am. Special thanks to my teachers and friends, Carmen Lacey and Hannelore. Thanks to all of you. Your work has had a significant impact on my work. Your journey is my journey. Thank you. Special thanks to Oprah Winfrey for sharing her journey with her viewers, spawning my very own magical journey. Oprah gave me tools I never had before, creating opportunity for significant personal growth. Thank you, Oprah.

Heartfelt thanks to Gail Currie, my "twin cousin," for understanding me and my project. Thank you, Gail, for helping me edit my first draft, and for every single word of encouragement along the way. My sincerest thanks also to Dr. Anne Marie Evers for connecting with me in such a profound manner, supporting me with her affirmations, and generously writing the foreward to this book. Thank you to Graham Currie for his outstanding artwork on my cover and for the drawings in the book. Thanks also to all the helpful folks at iUniverse for their support and guidance.

Foreword
By Dr. Anne Marie Evers

It is my great pleasure and honor to write this foreward for Debra J. Suchy. *Bellowed Whispers* is totally inspiring and very interesting. Author Deb is a practicing, well-respected Reiki Master. She shares her journey of understanding people, angels, rocks, stones, nature, and animals in a very personal and compelling way. She encourages the reader to have an open heart and to be prepared to accept miracles on all levels.

I believe by sharing her personal message Deb also gives others permission to do the same - journeying back to who they really are. As she shares the details of her spiritual progress, the reader is gently, yet firmly brought back to the place of finding out and knowing who they are.

Angels - yes I, too believe in angel presence, so much that I have a beautiful, little Angel Chapel in my back yard at home. When Deb refers to power animals it reminds me of my very own special power animal, a gorgeous and powerful tiger that I named Number 22 who has taken me safely on many wonderful astral journeys. Deb also gives great ideas and tips on how to clean your precious stones and how to energize them. I know from personal experience just how very important the proper cleaning of precious stones is.

Deb gives credit to many authors for their writings and suggests that one should be open to read and consider new ideas, methods, and ways of thinking and being; while stressing it is the reader's own choice what to believe, think, say, accept or do. The author encourages the reader to further awaken to the wondrous possibilities of the Universe and to share their stories as she has.

Deb suggests we all have Spirit's power within to generate and activate healing in others, always giving credit to the Creator/God. She believes we can all be willing conduits for Universal healing and comforting power to flow through.

I feel the purpose of this book is to inspire you to nurture your own spirit within. And so it is! As a fellow author I know how important it is to attract and keep the reader's interest which I feel Deb has done so beautifully. This is a great book with much uplifting and interesting information. Obtain a copy and sit in your favorite chair with a cup of herbal tea or coffee and experience its positive energy. Enjoy!

Dr Anne Marie Evers, Radio Talk Show Host, Author,
Ordained Minister, Columnist.
www.annemarieevers.com

= Introduction =

Life is grand. I often feel that way and share this joyful expression with others. Life is also painful. It is this pain that thrust me forward in my own journey to be more of who I really am. I recall many false starts, perhaps better labelled as missed opportunities, before I reached the level of commitment I have to my journey today.

In college I met a fascinating young woman who was different from anyone else I knew. I was immediately drawn to her, until I suspected that she practiced Wicca; then I distanced myself from her as quickly as you can say "Magick." I did not yet understand what an amazing opportunity this may have been to learn more about our metaphysical world. Other odd things happened during this time in my life: I had a scary out-of-body experience one night; I couldn't wear a watch because as soon as I put one on it would stop ticking; I lived when the doctors declared I should have died. It was the late 1970s, and it was a very confusing time for me. I didn't have any understanding of the metaphysical world, so I didn't have the tools to make sense of the oddities I was experiencing.

Then, in about 1995, I was particularly moved when Oprah Winfrey had Marianne Williamson, author of *Return to Love* (1992), on her show. For me the book was about returning to our spiritual selves, our divine selves. I devoured the book like a malnourished child. Having tasted the possibility of filling that empty space within me, I looked for more. I dragged my husband and young children to church. It was not the right fit for us. I kept reading. I read Louise Hay's book *You Can Heal Your Life* (1984) twice. The first time I read it, I didn't even finish it. The ideas were so out of the ordinary for me that I couldn't relate. Besides, I had been very blessed to have outstanding parents and an amazing husband and children. What would someone like me have to heal? The answer was plenty, but I didn't know that at the time. The second time I read Louise's book, I was ready for the messages. It was then profoundly meaningful to me. My whole life began to make more sense. My journey, as I know it now, began. In 2005 my journey accelerated significantly as I found myself surrounded by my current teachers.

I am compelled to share that which comes from deep within me, and to share details of my progress in life. I was clearly guided by Universal Life Force Energy (by Spirit, by God, by All That Is) in the writing of this book. Most days the words flowed freely from my pen. As I inputted each chapter into my laptop, my heavenly helpers would shut down the program if my edits affected the meaning of a passage. As I worked with my first editor, this became so obvious that we would roar with laughter each time it happened.

It is my hope that anyone can read and enjoy this little book, even reluctant readers. Although it is a quick and easy read, each chapter has much to offer, and is likely worth a second, or even a third, read. The first half (or so) of each chapter is about an experience I have had related to my own spiritual journey. The second half is some very basic information related to one of the themes in the story. I emphasize that this information is basic, as entire books have been written by others on each of the topics. Consider this book an introduction to the topic, a sampling of the many possibilities you can explore as you continue your journey. Near the end of each chapter I recommend my favourite books on the topic. There is a complete listing of these books in the bibliography.

It is my deepest desire that this book inspire you to nurture your own spirit within. I trust that one or more of these stories will awaken you to a topic or tool you may have never considered before. Many tools, approaches, opportunities will be available to you throughout your lifetime. Some will resonate with you. Some will not. My truth is not necessarily your truth. As you begin to awaken to the possibilities of the Universe, you will know what rings true for you and what does not. I rarely dismiss a concept, because I know that as I grow and change I may have a new understanding or framework for understanding that concept. My understanding is ever-changing.

I believe you must find your own way in this journey. You are not alone. You are never alone. Spirit is with you and within you. I suggest that you read many different books, study with many different teachers, and surround yourself with others who are also on this journey. I hope that this book illuminates more questions than answers. If so, then it, and I, have served our purpose.

1. The Magic of Rocks and Crystals

= Magic Stones =

Marci has been my friend for almost twenty-five years; before she was my friend, she was my sister-in-law. Recently we were on a ski vacation together with our families in the Rocky Mountains. She took me to a rock and gem store, where we viewed and touched some of Mother Earth's most beautiful offerings. I was especially moved by the energy of a large, breathtakingly beautiful polished sphere of chrysocolla. Seeing that I was visibly moved by the energy, Marci asked me what I was feeling. I was so immersed in the sensory experience that I gave her a very vague answer. I told her I felt more grounded and that I could feel it everywhere. I felt like I had butterflies in my tummy. I felt it in my heart chakra . . . and, yes . . . in my solar plexus. It was so powerful I handed it off to Marci. She seemed a little disappointed when she remarked that all she felt in her hands was a little tingle.

I had felt my whole body tingle as I held it. My legs felt heavier and more solidly planted into Mother Earth. I felt a swoosh of energy move through my heart chakra. I felt dancing in my belly, somewhat like butterflies but lighthearted and gently exciting. I'm not exactly sure what I felt in my solar plexus, but the words "solar plexus" popped into my consciousness, and I know this stone touched this chakra in a significant way. The stone also became very hot in my hands. I was moved beyond words in that moment.

Later, when Marci and her family left the store for their long drive home, I returned my attention to this magnificent stone. I felt the energy and I was moved once again. So I asked Anna, the shopkeeper, about the properties of the stone. She described it briefly as three stones that grow together naturally in nature. It is more formally known as a mineral of secondary origin. She also mentioned that it was a chakra-balancing, calming stone with grounding properties. She then opened up a reference book for me to read more. I was amazed that the stone's metaphysical properties corresponded to what I had intuitively and physically felt. As I am increasingly able to trust my intuition, I am delighted when I see or read "tangible" proof of the messages I take in. I chose a smaller, more affordable chrysocolla stone to purchase.

= Rocks and Crystals =

I wish I had told Marci that it was wonderful that she felt a slight tingle in her hands from the stone. Frankly, I was so caught up in the magic of my own response that I didn't take the time to celebrate Marci's experience. Marci recently began her own spiritual journey. I want Marci to know that the tingle in her hands from the stone is a gift. She is opening up to this energy. This is to be celebrated! In fact, a "tingle" may have been all that stone had to offer her. Perhaps another stone may give her an experience more like the one I described for myself. Marci will find her own way, at her own pace. You will, too.

My experience tells me that stones need to be chosen with our hearts rather than with our heads. Our intellect may tell us that we need to work on a certain area of our body or on a particular emotion. That's a start; however, try holding the stone you are drawn to, and if you have any reaction (other than pain), it is likely a good stone for you. In addition, if the stone heats up in your hands, then in my experience this is most definitely a good stone for you. If you have two stones that you are particularly drawn to but can only buy one, you can ask your guides or angels to help you choose the stone that will serve your highest good at that time. Then trust the answer that first pops into your head.

Stones and crystals can give us direction as to where to place our focus for our own healing. The chakras that are affected by a stone you are drawn to may represent an area of your life that needs loving, healing energy. I am so mesmerized and grateful for the healing energy of crystals and rocks that my hubby jokingly calls me his Little Stoner. There is much to learn about rocks and crystals. Everything on this amazing planet of ours is made of energy, including rocks and crystals. They vibrate at different frequencies, as we do. Different vibrational frequencies result in different, and sometimes related, metaphysical properties of specific rocks and crystals. Metaphysical properties refer to special gifts available to you: clarity of mind, support for new beginnings, releasing what no longer serves, and many, many other possibilities. The color of the stones can be a clue to what area of the body they will support. Colors also vibrate at different frequencies. Our bodies have seven major energy centers, known as chakras (pronounced shaw-krus). Each chakra is a different color in its balanced state. Stones of the same color typically support chakras of the same color. I believe crystals can gently balance and realign chakras.

Crown

Brow

Throat

Heart
Solar Plexus
Sacral
Base

Chakra	Primary Color in its Balanced State	My Favorite Stone to Support Each Chakra
crown	white or violet	amethyst
brow	indigo blue	sodalite
throat	sky blue	angeltite
heart	pink or forest green	rose quartz
solar plexus	yellow	citrine
sacral	orange	carnelian
base	red	garnet

The Universe will reveal to you what you need to know as you need to know it. If you are drawn to rocks, I encourage you to take your time and enjoy the journey. If you are not drawn to rocks, then they may not be your thing. I have a dear friend who is very sensitive to many different types of energy. However, she claims that those who feel energy from rocks only do so because they expect to do so. She knows that energy is everywhere around us, yet she dismisses energy from rocks and crystals because she cannot feel it. Although she loves to wear them, perhaps rocks aren't her thing. Maybe she will discover their power in the future, or maybe she is simply not tuned in to that energy in this lifetime. Either way, I encourage you to explore your own relationship with rocks, and not judge others if they can feel energy that you do not.

Loving rocks and crystals will truly open up a whole new world of energy to you. They appear to be solid and nonliving. Yet in my experience they are energetically alive. I discovered that placing amethyst and rose quartz in the sun actually depletes their energy. I had been placing my large sphere of amethyst in the sunlight and moonlight, thinking I was providing nourishment for her. When I realized what I had done, I felt great empathy for her and took steps to heal her energy. That is how much I love my rocks.

Rocks and crystals require regular cleansing and recharging. Cleansing does not refer simply to washing the stones. It refers to clearing away heavy or dense energy that has been picked up along the way from those who touch the stones or from the environment. There appear to be many different ways to achieve the same results. The desired result is that your stones are cleansed of heavy or dense energy and recharged with the Universal Life Force Energy.

I cleanse my stones in one of the following ways:

- I smudge the stones with sage grass or an appropriate incense. Sage incense is very effective, but some people find the scent too strong. Pine, sandalwood, and cedarwood are all incenses suitable for clearing stones. You light the grass or incense, then blow out the flame. The smoke has a heavier, denser energy than air, so the heavier, denser energy attached to the stones then attaches itself to the smoke and is carried off. This happens because objects are attracted to other objects with the same vibrational frequencies. Smudge outdoors or in a space with two windows open, creating airflow that allows the heavy, dense energy to flow safely out, where it is cleansed, blessed, and purified by Mother Earth. You can smudge by holding the stone between two fingers and rolling the stream of smoke over and around the stone.

- I also hold the stones under running water, while giving thanks that they are being cleansed, blessed, and purified by the precious water from our beloved Mother Earth. The words that I choose are much less important than my intention for this to occur.

When recharging stones, I always ask the Universe, "Please re-energize these beautiful stones from Mother Earth so that they may serve their highest purpose and help me to serve my highest purpose." I immediately give thanks, as if the recharging has already occurred; in this way, love and appreciation flows to the stones and to the Universe. Then I recharge my stones. My favorite ways to recharge my stones are:

- Hold the stones in my left hand, while using the fire finger (middle finger) on my right hand to create Reiki symbols over the stones. You need to have Reiki in order to use this method. This method cleanses and recharges simultaneously.

- Place the stones in soil or snow in sunlight and moonlight for one to two days. This is especially effective around the energy of the full moon.

The sun need not be shining brightly and the full moon may even be hidden by clouds; their healing energy is still present. Be advised, however, that direct sunlight may damage jewelry that is strung together with elastic or fishing line, as these substances may break down in the heat. Also, amethyst and rose quartz do not like the sunlight. Most stones are not affected by the cold, but certain opals should not be placed in extreme cold. My experience is that the birds leave the stones alone, and I have been told that if a stone disappears, then it is not intended for you at that time. However, when it comes to my most precious stones, like the diamond anniversary ring my husband gave me, I don't take any chances that a magpie might need it more than I. I hang it securely on a chain in the sunlight and moonlight.

- You can also place the stones in unrefined sea salt for several days. This is a very effective tool; however, this process stripped my angelite of its polished finish. I assumed that the stone was more powerful in its more natural state for me at that time. This process does not normally strip a stone of its polished finish, but may do so with certain stones. The sea salt absorbs any dense or heavy energy accumulated in the stone; therefore the sea salt must be cleansed periodically. One way to do this is to set your intention that the sea salt be cleansed, blessed, and purified by Mother Earth. Then cup your hands, scooping a handful of the salt and holding one cupped hand higher than the other. Let the salt flow from the higher hand to the lower hand while gentle breezes flow through it, cleansing it. Repeat this process until you sense that the sea salt has been cleansed.

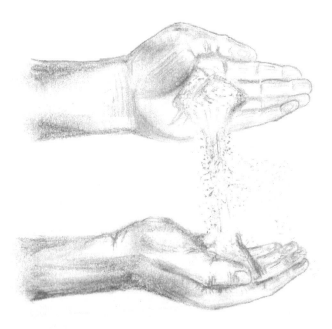

- I also discovered that you can recharge your stones with the powerful energy drawn by a pyramid. It has been suggested that after cleansing your stones you can place them under a pyramid; then, through your intention or with Reiki symbols, the Universe will recharge them in as little as thirty seconds. Beautiful pyramids made of colored glass or a variety of other materials are commercially available. You can also create your own pyramid out of craft wire in order to harness this powerful energy.

After cleansing your stones, you can wear them next to your body. You may choose to wear them as jewelry, stuff them into your pockets, or wear them in a pouch hung around your neck. Some crystals can also be placed in your space for protection or healing. For example, some believe a piece of black tourmaline placed near your computer will protect you from harmful radiation give off by your computer. The size of a stone is not important, as a tiny stone may be just as powerful as a large stone.

There is much, much more for you to learn. I recommend that you get acquainted with the staff at your local rock and gem store. They can be a wonderful resource for you.

There are also many books that you may find helpful. Two of my favorite introductory books on this topic are Judy Hall's *The Illustrated Guide to Crystals* (2000) and Melody's *Love Is in the Earth: A Kaleidoscope of Crystals* (2005). I invite you to explore the magic of rocks and crystals for yourself.

2. Laying on of Hands for Healing

= Mom, Come Do Your Voodoo Thing =

During a Seven Sisters Gathering Circle in our home, my daughter Madison, stood at the French doors and called to me, "Mom, come do your voodoo thing." I giggled nervously and quietly left the room where my friends were gathered. I wasn't sure if the newest members of our group would be comfortable if they thought I might use voodoo in any way. I went to Madison immediately, partly because I was thrilled that she was acknowledging my healing gifts, and partly because I didn't want her to say voodoo again.

As I suspected, my daughter had an injured bird in her cupped hands. It had flown into a window, fallen to the veranda floor, and had been scooped up by our dog, Charlie. Madison had rescued this little one right out of his mouth. She brought the little bird to me for healing. She and I had rescued small birds before. She physically rescues them, places them on the palm of her hand, and then, through me, the Universe makes the healing energy of Reiki available to them.

I will always remember the first time we teamed up this way. Early one morning, I walked into Madison's room, and there she stood with a little bird in the palm of her hand. She looked like Cinderella, standing in her attic bedroom talking to this little bird on her outstretched palm. The little one had hit her bedroom window and fallen to the roof below. Madison had opened her window and picked it up. I placed my healing Reiki hands over it. The little bird recovered fully within a few minutes, Madison set it on the window ledge, and it flew away. Madison indicated to me that she thought the bird was simply dazed and would have been okay, with or without Reiki. At that time, I honestly thought that was probably true.

Next time the Universe made it more obvious that Reiki played a role in the recovery. Madison and I were in the yard, playing with our critters, when Madison discovered that one of our cats had a tiny bird in his mouth. The cat dropped the bird and Charlie picked it up. Madison commanded him to drop it. She reached for the obviously injured little bird, then held it in her open palm while I offered the healing energy of Reiki from the Universe. When the bird appeared to be okay, Madison tried launching it into flight off the palm of her hand. It would not go. So she continued to hold the little one and I continued to give Reiki. She tried launching the bird again. Once again, it stayed. It drew more healing energy through my hands. On Madison's third attempt to launch this little one into flight, it flew a short distance at first, then disappeared into the sky.

So on the day Madison called me to the French doors for yet another injured bird, I was not surprised. Sadly, though, this one was dying. I believe it came to us for the comfort we could provide. Yet again Madison held a tiny life in the palm of her hands, and yet again I placed my Reiki hands over this precious life. As the little one's breathing settled, it stood up briefly, flapped its wings, and then gave one big last breath and passed on. I gave a blessing and we said good-bye.

Many weeks later, at a family gathering at my brother's home, once again a bird hit a window. And once again, Madison rescued the bird. Madison and I settled into our familiar roles; she with the bird on her palm and me offering Reiki healing energy through my hands. The bird healed, and after several attempts to launch it into flight, it flew away. I walked back into the house where others had been watching through the picture window. Some family members politely asked me about what I had done, and one, in particular, expressed genuine interest in talking more about Reiki. So we did. Many months later, at a family wedding, a cousin who had shown very little interest in the topic of Reiki and the little bird at the time shared with me that he was particularly moved by the healing. Thank you, little bird.

= Reiki =

Despite what my daughter says, Reiki (pronounced "ray-key") is not voodoo. To me Reiki is sacred. It is a powerful way to access Universal Life Force Energy. Through Reiki I am able to experience pure, loving, healing energy from our Creator. This energy surrounds us. Indeed, it sustains us. Yet we get bogged down in our daily lives, and we may be unaware of this love around us and within us. Often the energy in our physical bodies is so blocked that the Universal Life Force Energy cannot flow freely; this often results in dis-ease or illness (Hay, 1987). I believe we cannot truly be whole if this energy is not flowing within us and around us. Reiki is one way I choose to access Universal Life Force Energy. It is an ancient form of hands-on healing.

I am most familiar with the Usui method of Reiki. Those who use the Usui System of Natural Healing are taught that Reiki is an ancient healing art from Tibet. Apparently it was rediscovered by Dr. Mikao Usui in the late 1800s. It is reported that Dr. Usui studied at a Zen monastery under an elderly abbot for seven years. Upon discovering the symbols and methods for this healing, Dr. Usui retreated to a mountain to gain the power needed to heal. As the story goes, this sacred information was passed on to Dr. Hayashi, who was committed to serving others. Dr. Hayashi had a clinic in Tokyo, where Hawayo Takata was treated and recovered from a brain tumor. Mrs. Takata, who was from Hawaii, returned home with the knowledge and understanding of Reiki. Mrs. Takata's granddaughter, Phyllis Furumoto, became a Reiki Master in 1980. She passed her knowledge along to a highly regarded Reiki Master and author, William Rand, among many others. Each Usui Reiki Master can track his or her lineage back to Dr. Mikao Usui (Stein, 1995).

I am a Reiki Master. This means that I am able to pass attunements and teach others about Reiki. There are three levels in this system. Level I is primarily for self-healing. The Reiki Master uses a series of powerful symbols and movements, known as an attunement, to open up students' energy to the possibilities of the Universe. In Level I, students explore the principles of Reiki, its benefits, its history, and how it works. They also learn to give themselves a treatment.

They may or may not be given the first symbol, known as cho-ku-rei, which is often described as the symbol used to switch on the Reiki.

In Level II, students receive one to two more attunements, further increasing the energy flow between the Source and the receiver. Three Reiki symbols are shared and practiced, enhancing the healing energy. Students learn to give Reiki treatments to others.

Level III is intended for those who wish to teach others about Reiki, in addition to giving treatments. There are two more attunements, increasing students' ability to channel healing. The method of passing attunements is shared and practiced. Additional symbols are passed on. Information from all three levels is reviewed and teaching methods are discussed. After teaching and passing attunements, the student becomes a Master.

Reiki practitioners are taught to ask permission from the client before giving or sending Reiki. A practitioner can connect with the higher self of anyone who is not able to speak for him- or herself and achieve permission this way.

A Reiki treatment typically takes place with the client fully clothed on a professional massage table. The client has as many cozy blankets as s/he chooses. Ideally the room has soft lighting, candles burning, essential oils in the air, and soft music in the background. The Reiki practitioner calls upon Universal Life Force Energy, his/her Reiki Masters, Healing Masters, and all those beings of light of the highest vibration who wish to come forward and help in the healing. The practitioner then lays his/her hands over the major energy points in the client's body. Then, as if by magic, the energy flows. The practitioner is simply a conduit for this energy; the client draws in the energy. The practitioner is not sending energy, nor is s/he exchanging his/her own energy with the client. The practitioner is grounded and shielded, and does not take on any dis-ease from the client. The practitioner's hands usually become very warm or hot as his/her hands are laid over the client's body. Sometimes a practitioner will snap fingers, clap hands, ring a prayer bowl, or use a drum or rattle to break up dense energy in the client's energy field that may be blocking the flow of Universal Life Force Energy. Clients typically feel an enormous sense of relaxation, peace, or love. Some clients are moved to tears. Others see colors in their mind's eye. Some feel odd sensations in their bodies. Still others only feel relaxation.

The client must be a willing partner in this process. Individuals can block this flow of energy. They may not be ready for healing. There may be more they have to learn from their discomfort or dis-ease before healing can occur. You see, I believe our bodies are continually giving us messages to assist us in our learning. If we don't listen, the messages become more and more intense, until dis-ease forces us to listen. I highly recommend Louise Hay's work in this area. Her book *You Can Heal Your Life* was life-changing for me.

I believe Reiki can change the chemical balance and structure of the body by helping to regenerate organs, rebuild tissue, and create emotional balance. Essentially, I believe Reiki helps the body heal itself. I also strongly believe that Reiki should not be used in place of standard medical treatment, but in addition to treatment. It will not interfere with medical treatment, with one exception that I am aware of. I was taught not to give Reiki to someone with a broken bone before the bone is set, because Reiki will speed the healing and it is not desirable for healing to occur before the bone is set into the correct position.

Reiki is a truly precious gift to give yourself and others. For me Reiki is so very sacred that I choose to prepare myself and my space as if I am giving a client a treatment. Then

I soak up the Reiki from my own hands and the etherical hands of all those beings of the highest vibration who are there to assist me. This process is intensely spiritual and private. Some of my practical friends simply switch on the Reiki while watching TV or chatting with friends and invite the healing energy in. Both approaches result in increased flow of loving energy.

Reiki can be shared with people, animals, and plants. You can use it to bless your food. You can send it long-distance. Reiki is truly amazing. If you want to learn more about Reiki, I recommend that you read Diane Stein's *Essential Reiki: A Complete Guide to an Ancient Healing Art* (1995). Seek out a Reiki Master you trust to teach you and then join or create a Reiki circle. My Reiki circle was a group of women with different levels of Reiki. We met once per week. We practiced giving each other treatments, each receiving our own treatment. This was a phenomenal way to learn and to increase our own capacity to channel energy.

One of my most profound moments in this journey was the moment I truly understood that we are all connected. It was no longer an intellectual understanding of the science behind the concept. I *felt* it deep within my being. I *knew* it to be my truth. It was in that moment that I embraced the knowledge that healing myself actually helps others heal, because we are all connected. We can help the children and adults in our own lives heal. We can help children and adults around the world heal. We can help our Mother Earth heal. We can do this by simply doing our own healing, our own work. As we heal, our energetic vibration increases, and others benefit. It is not our role to fix or heal others. Even when we give Reiki to others, we are not doing the healing, we are simply the conduit through which the receivers are accessing Universal Life Force Energy in order to do their own healing. We can only heal ourselves, but we can make the world a better place by doing so.

3. Animal Totems

= Namaste, Baby Moose =

Moose gently wandered into my life. At first, I didn't even know they were there for me, not in that way. They had to leave and return before I really noticed our connection.

We live in the country, and for years we had a cow and bull moose living across the road in the bush. I suspect they got tired of dealing with our dogs invading their space and left our area. Moose are grand creatures, huge in stature, with long, lanky legs and broad chests. They are as awkward as they are beautiful. I missed their oddly magnificent presence. I was delighted when they returned.

Then in January, while on a ski trip, I discovered an irresistible moose ornament. She was about five inches tall. The little moose was personified as an awkwardly sexy cowgirl in a red skirt, hat, and boots. Seeing her made me laugh out loud. I bought her and hung her in my red vehicle, which I declared be known as "Moose" from that day forward. Every time I hop into Moose, I see the little figurine hanging from the rearview mirror and I smile.

I did not yet see the pattern that was unfolding. In mid-January, I was upset to see that one of our dogs had carried home the bottom portion of an ankle and hoofed foot. Based on the size and color, it was clearly from a baby moose. I was shocked. I realized that the body part was frozen and there was no way our dogs had killed this precious baby, because they had been in the barn all night. Still, I was sad. I had the unsettling sense that this little one had somehow given its life so that I would take notice of whatever it was the Universe was trying to tell me. I wanted to believe that the baby must have been stillborn. I will never know for sure. I did know in my heart, however, that it was no coincidence that this baby moose's ankle and hoof had made their way to me.

So I read about moose and welcomed the message that having moose appear in your life indicates that you are emotionally stronger than you realize. This message came to me at a critical time, bringing me hope and comfort. I was very, very grateful.

Two weeks passed. I was on my way into the city. I was totally focused on my driving as I maneuvered Moose through a sharp curve. At first I didn't see them. They were on the edge of some trees no more than fifteen feet off the road: three of the largest, most magnificent moose I had ever seen. I couldn't believe my eyes. I shook my head. I looked again. They were really there. I surrounded them with light for their safety and the safety of other drivers. I admitted to myself that the unshakeable feeling that the baby moose had more to say was real, not imagined.

Two months passed. It was then spring. I was keenly aware that moose had more messages for me, but I had no idea what they were. One day, during a past-life regression in which my intention was to dispel fear that was blocking me from being All That I Am, I had the following experience:

> I found myself as a huge male moose standing in a marshy area of the woods. It was peaceful and serene. I could see myself, as this magnificent moose, reach down deep into the marsh and surface with a mouthful of greens. The green vegetation was hanging out the sides of my mouth, as the water ran out of the corners and down the protruding greens. The picture was vivid. I was slow moving and comfortable in my environment. My message from me, as this moose, to my current me, was precise and clear. The message

was: "You are strong. There is no need to be afraid of
being who you are. All that happened in the past is in
the past. Don't be afraid. There is only light."

Then, the following May, I had a lomilomi massage treatment
with two gifted healers from Hawaii. Lomilomi is an ancient
healing art. Later, in an e-mail sent to me on June 29, 2008,
Lyn Fehr described lomilomi as a "flowing, nurturing form
of massage based on an ancient, shamanic rite of passage
that was originally designed to enlighten the being in the
physical body." During this otherworldly experience, I invited
moose medicine to come fully into my life. In my mind's eye,
I had the sense that moose energy was above me. It was as
if I could see the space between the particles that made up
moose; the kind of space that Eckhart Tolle writes about in
A New Earth (2005). I was keenly aware, for the first time
ever, that I, too, was space, interspersed with particles. The
particles of this moose were merged with my being. We were
one once again, and I was fully aware of it. Hallelujah!

= Moose Medicine =

Moose is an ancient power totem; it is a symbol of courage
and determination. I call on moose often for courage. I

define courage as moving forward even when I am afraid. Moose are found in the north of the medicine wheel, which represents wisdom. At the root of moose medicine is an understanding of the wisdom of silence; so when words are spoken, they are to be spoken with pride. Self-esteem is the medicine of the moose because it represents the power in acknowledging that wisdom was utilized in a situation and is to be appreciated, even celebrated. Thank you, moose.

Bull moose's powerful bellow symbolizes joyful expression of accomplishments. It is not boastful but comes from deep within our highest selves. This bellow can be heard for many miles, signifying that our presence is known to all when necessary. And yet moose can camouflage themselves and can move quickly and silently through the forest. Those of us who are aligned with moose can blend into our environment; can become invisible when it's necessary. The magnificent antlers of moose are like antennae; by extension, we can receive spiritual messages and strengthen our intuition. Their antlers protect them during battle; we can learn to shield ourselves with our truth and spiritual understanding. According to Sams and Carson's *Medicine Cards: The Discovery of Power Through the Ways of the Animals* (1999):

Moose medicine people have the ability to know when to use the gentleness of Deer and when to activate the stampede of Buffalo. They understand the balance between giving orders to get things done and having a willingness to do things themselves. The wisdom of Moose medicine is akin to the Grandfather Warrior who has long since put away his war paint and is now advising young bucks to cool their blood. . . . Moose medicine is often found in elders who have walked the Good Red Road and have seen many things in their Earth walk. Their joy lies in being the teacher of the children, and in being the first ones to give encouragement. . . . The elders are honored in tribal law for their gifts of wisdom, for their teaching abilities and for the calmness they import. (81–82)

Sams and Carson even go on to suggest that those aligned with moose should "write down their progress in life and share it with others" (82). This fascinates me. It is said that one does not align with moose; rather, moose aligns with you. That has been my truth. Moose gently entered my life, helping me to remember who I really am. I was compelled to write about my journey long before I read Sams and Carson's book. I knew I was comfortable as a leader and as a follower, long before I understood moose energy. I am equally at ease blending into a group and standing out in a group. I know in my heart I am a teacher. And yet, knowing moose is within me and understanding more about moose energy affirms that I am on the path to becoming more of All That I Am.

I have other animal totems that I love dearly and call upon for guidance and support. Animals are so very loving. I believe they will actually take on our pain and dis-ease so that we may heal. Some animals, like dolphins and horses, have a very high vibration; it is healing simply to be in their presence. Birds and reptiles can also bring us understanding or warn us of dangers. I have many more stories to tell about how animals have brought joy and awareness into my life. Most of these stories are not as mysterious as my moose medicine journey, but they are no less profound.

If you are drawn to a certain animal or find that a certain animal keeps showing up in your life, that animal may be one of your spirit guides. Mother Earth kindly sends us messages, often through animals. Two of my favorite resources for understanding what animal guides have to offer and what it means when they show up in our lives are Ted Andrews's *Animal Speak: The Spiritual and Magical Powers of Creatures Great and Small* (1993) and Steven Farmer's *Animal Spirit Guides* (2006).

I invite you to welcome animal energy into your life. Notice what these animals are offering you, and let them know you are grateful. I am especially grateful to baby moose, because his gift to me was profound. I was forever awakened to this powerful energy. Namaste, baby moose, namaste.

4. Angels among Us

= My Angel, My Teacher =

I often refer to my son as my angel. There are many reasons why. I recall one distinct moment in time when he and I knelt by his bed to pray. He clasped his tiny hands tightly; although he was barely walking, he knelt solidly next to me. It had been quite some time since we had prayed together. Partway through the brief prayer, he suddenly burst into tears. In my heart I could hear him say, "Oh, God! There You are. I have missed You so." He did not speak these words, but the message was clear to me. I held my son as we wept quietly together.

Later, when my son was about three years old, we were at the front door preparing to leave the house for the day. He was giving me a really hard time. I was running late and was increasingly frustrated. Finally, I sat on the stairs and pulled him into my lap to ask him what was wrong. He told me that he felt like he didn't belong. My heart sank, as both of my children are adopted, and I have always wanted them to understand how deeply they are loved by their father and me, and by their birthparents. I didn't want to assume that I knew what he meant, so I asked him, "Do you feel like you don't belong in our family . . . in your playschool . . . at your daycare?" and then out of the blue I added, ". . . on this planet?" He replied ever so quietly and matter-of-factly, "On this planet." I can't recall exactly how I responded, but I remember telling him to let me know when he had those feelings again. Over the next several weeks he would announce to me, "Mom, I have that feeling again." I would simply acknowledge that I heard him, and he would whiz by me to run off to play. For a while I was afraid that he was an angel who would only be on our planet for a short time.

As the years pass, I worry less about my son leaving our planet prematurely and have come to understand that he is one of my greatest teachers in this lifetime. He and I have a profound and intimate connection that I am eternally grateful for. And yet, as he grows into a man, he needs to push me away in order to be more of who he is. One day, when I was feeling especially rejected by and disconnected from him, he sent me a message to remind me that even though he is an angel, he is still on his own journey. As I was driving into town, I was playing a CD that he had made for me. One line in one song skipped, playing repeatedly over and over several times. The line was, "God knows, sometimes even angels fall." That CD had never skipped before that moment and has never skipped again. It was then that I clearly understood—he must find his own way.

= Angels =

I have always thought of my son as my angel; I have never thought of myself as one. That is, until recently. During a Reiki treatment with a dear friend and mentor, I saw my own wings for the very first time. It was virtually unbelievable, and if it weren't for the synchronicities that followed I may have dismissed what I saw. As I lay on my back on the massage table with my eyes closed, my friend handed me crystals to hold in each hand. I immediately felt light-headed, as if my energy was bouncing around the room. Then I had the sensation that my energy was flying around the room. I have always loved this feeling, and I experience the ultimate thrill when I find myself flying in my dreams. As delightful as this sensation was, my friend and I both knew intuitively that I needed to ground. Assuming I was safely grounded into Mother Earth, we continued. As I slipped into a deeper state of relaxation, in my mind's eye I saw a figure standing before me in space. I couldn't tell if the figure was a man or a woman, but as I looked closer I saw that it was a precious angel with breathtakingly beautiful wings. The wings appeared to be almost the full height of the angel. They were feathered wings. As I struggled to see this angel more clearly, I realized that this angel was ME. In that same instant, my friend commanded me to breathe my higher self in. As I focused on my breathing, the angel disappeared and I immediately began to question my declaration that it was me.

As I lay there doubting what I thought had just happened, I began to sense something under me on the massage table. At first I just squirmed a little; then, I lifted my shoulders and upper back up from the table. I was lying on my wings! Oh my God! I could see and feel my own wings.

This did not make any sense to me, because as I understood it, humans could not be angels. Angels could appear as humans to help someone in a crisis, but according to Sylvia Browne in *Phenomenon* (2005), humans and angels are different species. Sylvia believes that angels never incarnate as humans. So, as vivid and amazing as this experience was, hours later I began to doubt what I had seen and felt.

Then the synchronicities began to occur. For no reason at all, my sister-in-law gave me a lovely heart-shaped resin piece with a beautiful ivory angel inside. I walked into my favorite rock and gem shop, where I was drawn to a lovely pale blue stone that I had never seen before. It was angelite. My son gave me three angels: two crystal angels for the Christmas tree and one on a pewter key chain with the engraved words, "My guardian angel is watching over me." There was no special occasion. He simply gave them to me.

Could it be true? Am I an angel? I cannot ignore what I saw and felt, and yet my ego would not allow me to think of myself in that way. I am as special as each and every one of God's creations, but I am human, with human traits and struggles. With great curiosity, tempered with skepticism, I began to read about angels.

In Phenomenon, Sylvia Browne clearly states that angels never incarnate as human beings, because they are two different species. She believes angels can take on human form to assist us here, but that this event is very brief. As soon as the angel has served its divine purpose in that moment, the angel in human form disappears as quickly as it appeared. She says that angels are androgynous, not exclusively male or female. She describes them as exquisitely beautiful, with illuminated skin, transcending and including all races. I have great respect for Sylvia Browne's work. I believe that she is not necessarily right or wrong. This is her reality. My experience, however, tells me that it may be possible for angels to incarnate as humans. I, too, have a sense that angels are balanced in male and female energy. I, too, sense their exquisite beauty. When I feel their presence or see them in my mind's eye, I am always moved to tears.

I do believe, as Sylvia Browne does, that they communicate with us telepathically. One day I became aware of one of my angels who is here on this planet to support me. When I asked for my angel's name, the series of sounds that came by way of reply was unrecognizable to me. So I blurted out, "What was that?" In a playful tone, my angel said to me, "You can just call me Daniel." I believe they show themselves to us and communicate with us in ways that we can understand. I don't know whether angels are simply exquisite balls of light or if they actually resemble humans with spectacular wings. I do know that when I saw myself as an angel, I was neither male nor female. I was exquisitely beautiful, and my pure white feathered wings were the full height of my body. That is not proof to me that angels look like that. It simply tells me that my mind presented this image to me in a form I would understand.

I have a very powerful example of how the Universe provides

us with images that are recognizable to us. It is not a story about angels. In fact, this is a story about heavy, dense energy. One day I was doing a meditation, intending to clear away layers of fear. In my mind's eye, I saw a dark, heavy, shapeless cloud. It became denser and heavier, still having no particular shape. Then it growled at me! This frightened me, and my brain instantaneously began to try to make sense of what was happening. In my mind's eye, the cloud began to take shape. I could see tiny blocks of color, like mega-pixels, being rearranged into a form recognizable to me. You may have seen this happen on a television screen when the satellite signal fades, then recovers. I was in awe of this process unfolding in my mind. It happened very quickly. Then it was over. The new image was a vicious, three-headed dog. I recognized this represented fear to me. I thanked the fear for serving me, surrounded it in light, and released it to the Universe to be cleansed, blessed, and purified.

In *Earth Angels* (2002), Doreen Virtue describes earth angels as souls, originating from the same source as others, but not originating from planet Earth. She writes that earth angels typically have passion and gifts for helping others through healing or teaching, and yet they have their own earthly challenges. She says earth angels are very sensitive and despise violence. They often feel like they don't belong here. This rings true for me. Every time I read Doreen's book I cry softly, appreciating that at last I feel understood.

Doreen says that not everyone is an earth angel. She explains that some human beings are here simply for their own learning or enjoyment. Their lives are committed to human concerns. Conversely, earth angels are here primarily to assist with the much-anticipated shift in human consciousness, sometimes known as the New Age of Peace.

I believe that I likely am an earth angel. This does not make me any more or less special than anyone or anything. It just is. Spirit is within each of us. This is my truth, for now. I am open to new learning and insights as my journey unfolds. I encourage you to read more about angels. Angels can help us in many ways. We have all heard stories where angels save people. They can also help with small, everyday matters. With grace and gratitude, I often send my angels ahead to clear a parking space for me. It works. One day I was looking for a recipe for a plain white cake, and I asked my guides and angels for assistance. I closed my eyes and reached into the cupboard. I pulled out a book of sugarless recipes. At first I rejected the idea that this particular book would have such a recipe. Then I paused, realizing that this was the book my guides and angels directed me to. So, trusting that they responded to my intention, I flipped through the book and found the recipe. I laughed out loud when I realized the recipe was actually called "Plain Cake," which is exactly what I had asked for. I thanked my guides and angels as I danced my happy dance in the kitchen.

Angels may come to us in many forms. They are part of our spiritual support system. I invite you to know and enjoy the angels around you. When the time is right, you will find your own truth in your own way.

5. Healing Through Past Lives

= Anna's Story =

Dear, sweet, simple Anna thought she could protect her baby. She carried her baby girl in a giant sling, which hung from her left shoulder across her body and over her right hip. Her baby had grown into a toddler, hanging day after day, week after week, month after month on her mother's hip. Anna and her baby were outcasts. Anna felt dirty. Unclean. Her own father hated her because she bore his child.

Anna was younger than her years. She looked different from other girls her age. Her forehead was very deep. Her facial shape was squared and her eyes were set wide apart. Her body was rounded and frumpy. Many thought of her as a nothing, as no one. But Anna was Baby's mother. Baby was not named, but Baby was loved. Anna did not understand why she and her baby were dirty, but she understood that she needed to protect her baby. Sadly, Baby was never able to leave her mother's hip to play or to explore her world.

Then one day Anna and her baby were alone in the courtyard hanging laundry out to dry. Anna was chatting quietly to Baby, and Baby was cooing back at her. A large shadow darkened the courtyard. It was Anna's father. She looked deeply into his eyes, and his face was etched into her memory forever as he struck her on her hip where Baby sat. He struck her with a bamboo cane, again and again and again, until the young mother and her baby lay in a broken heap on the ground. As their spirits left their bodies, Anna cried out to Baby that she was sorry, that she had tried to protect her and she was sorry that she had failed. It broke her heart to have failed her baby.

Anna carried that energy into each of her next lifetimes. As me in the twenty-first century, she lives a charmed life in the country with my loving husband and children. I am loving, intelligent, creative, and joyful. I am a far more knowledgeable and capable mother than I was as Anna, and yet I love my children no less deeply and profoundly than Anna loved Baby. Anna lives within me. I feel her pain.

I experienced pain in my right hip that became increasingly unbearable. During a past-life regression I recalled Anna's story and recognized Anna's father's face as a young man from my current lifetime. I also recognized Baby as my daughter from this lifetime. During the past-life regression Baby told me (as Anna) that Baby knows Anna did her best to protect her. Sweet, simple trusting Anna immediately released the pain. Simultaneously, I healed in this lifetime, too. My hip pain, where I (as Anna) had carried Baby for so many months, and where she had been so savagely beaten, was gone. Upon reflection, I remembered that years earlier another healer had described the stuck energy on my right hip as a baby's energy.

In this lifetime, I had not borne my own children. They made their way to me and my husband through adoption at birth. I wonder if this stuck energy had been released lifetimes ago, whether I might have felt worthy enough to bear my own children in this lifetime. All that matters to me is that my children did make their way to us. For that, and so much more, I will always be grateful.

Past-Life Regression

Past-life regression has been a powerful tool in my journey to be All That I Am. While I will do much of my own self-healing work using other techniques, I believe past-life work needs to be done with a trusted, experienced guide. You need to be safely in the moment, immersed in your journey; a willing participant in the process.

Prior to my session, I identify the issue or pain that I wish to clear. I write down my intention. It usually goes something like this, "I, Debra Jean Connery Suchy, intend to go back to the very first time the seed was planted that resulted in . . . " I take this to the session with me, and the healer restates the intention to commence the process. Then I trust that Spirit will take me exactly where I need to go. I lie quietly on a massage table or on a mat on the floor. I remain aware of the environment around me, which fades into the background, as I become increasingly relaxed. I keep my eyes closed. Through this facilitated process, I enter into an altered state of consciousness, where I am exceptionally relaxed but totally aware of my thoughts.

The facilitator guides me to connect with my inner child and safely place her into a beautiful protective ball of light. My inner child is so active in, and familiar with, the routine that she usually just climbs right up into the ball. We establish a signal so that if my inner child is frightened in any way she can let me know. Her signal to me is that she will tickle my nose and it will start to itch. This trust is crucial to the process; both you and your inner child must feel safe in order to move forward in this journey. The adult "you" may want to do this, but the child in you may be fearful.

My mind becomes quieter; my breathing, deep and rhythmic. In my mind's eye, I begin to see my journey back in time as facilitated by the healer I am working with. The healer may use one of many different "vehicles" to take me back. My favorite is the "River of Time." This is where the healer invites me to climb into a boat or canoe that floats along the river of time.

When I arrive at the point in time where the seed was first planted that resulted in the issue or pain, the story unfolds. The Universe gifted me with sight, so I see the story unfold in my mind's eye. I also have a sense of knowing. I don't usually hear words being spoken; rather, I know what has been spoken. In my experience, the charge that resulted in the pain or issue occurred as a trauma in a past life. This charge follows us into each subsequent life time until it is healed. The charge is created through our need to heal unresolved or suppressed emotions around the trauma, so understandably, revisiting this trauma may be emotional. It is important to remain an observer of the event. A good facilitator will help you to stay in your observer role and will guide you through significant exercises to help you understand and heal the trauma. This powerful process works because it allows you to get to the underlying issue rather than focusing on the symptoms. The most amazing result of past-life regression therapy is that your profound healing may create healing backward and forward in your genetic lineage. Yes, by healing your neck pain you may heal your parent's and/or your child's neck pain. In fact, I have seen it happen. Isn't that amazing? These miracles are our birthright.

Past-life regression can also be used to go back in time to reclaim lost talents and gifts. My dear friend Tara went back in time to bring back knowledge about creating medicine from plants and herbs. Tara's sense of knowing and trusting Mother Earth to give her what she needs to create her salves and sprays is inspiring. Her business is also thriving.

How do you trust that what you have seen, heard, or felt during a regression was real? You may experience a deep sense of "knowing" that resonates with you. You simply know it is true.

You may also experience synchronicities that confirm your knowing. A synchronicity occurs when you notice two or more events that appear to be a coincidence when in actuality the linking of the events has significance. There really are no random coincidences, only meaningful coincidences, known as synchronicities. For example, during one of my very first past-life regressions, I doubted what I saw and felt. I saw a landscape and dwellings I had never seen before, not even on television. I saw clothing that was totally unfamiliar to me. A date popped into my head that didn't make any sense to me at all. Yet even with all my doubts, I had a knowing deep within me. A quirky series of events unfolded immediately after my session, and within an hour I found myself unexpectedly sitting in my favorite bookstore. My usual armchair was not available, so I had to sit in another area, an area I would never normally have chosen. As I sat there, consumed with thoughts of the session, a book caught my eye. It was about Greece, which was where I found myself during the past-life regression. It was a children's book, full of illustrations. I opened it up and was amazed to find a timeline, with the date I had remembered in the session. It matched the date given for dwellings and clothing similar to the ones I had seen in my session. That synchronicity told me that what I remembered was real. My memory had been historically accurate, which validated my sense of knowing.

Past-life regressions are a powerful way to heal ourselves and others. This is simply a snapshot of the possibilities to encourage you to read about and experience past-life regressions firsthand with a trusted healer. Your time to heal is now. The first book I read on the topic was Browne's *Past Lives, Future Healing*. It was an excellent introduction to the topic for me. I also recommend *Past Lives, Present Miracles* (2008), by Denise Linn, for further exploration.

6. Traveling through Time and Space

= Crossing Over =

I sat in the sun, wrapped in the arms of Mother Earth as my Reiki Master, Carmen, began my attunement. When I felt my dad's energy, I was pleased. When I felt my uncle's energy, I was confused. My dad is living. His brother, my uncle, has passed over. Why were their spirits here together?

My thoughts turned to them. My father is living, yet somehow he sometimes manages to show up during my healing sessions. Though my Uncle Jim and I did not spend a lot of time together in this lifetime, I was able to visit him during his last hours on this planet. I believe the Reiki that passed through me into him during that time brought him comfort, and eased some of his fear of passing. Later he crossed over safely to his beloved ones, surrounded by his loving children and grandchildren.

I tried to turn my focus back to the moment. Suddenly, I panicked! I felt sick to my stomach. I couldn't breathe. I wondered if my father, who is unwell, had suddenly died. I wondered if he and Uncle Jim had come to tell me. Bravely, I pushed away the fear and realized that was not why they were here.

My attunement continued. I focused on being in the moment. I could hear a hawk in the distance. I could feel the energy shifting. At some point, in my mind's eye, my father's spirit offered to take a huge dark mass of pain from my heart chakra. Once again, I was confused. I couldn't let him do that, because he is battling heart disease. I couldn't let him take on additional burdens. And yet I wondered if I was supposed to accept this gift, given in much love.

My attunement was complete. I thanked the Universe. I stood up. I smiled and thanked my dear friend and Reiki Master. My mind and body were moving slowly. I felt dazed. My head was throbbing. I needed to communicate further with my father. I also needed to know why my uncle was here. I quietly stepped away from the group. I sat on the steps in the front yard. In my mind's eye, Dad was still insisting that he could take this pain from me. Shaking my head, I sobbed out loud, telling him with my thoughts, "No. I am stronger now. I can do it myself. All I need to do is surround the pain with light, then send it off to the Universe to be cleansed, blessed, and purified. I can do this, Dad."

Before I knew it, it was done. I had released the dense, painful energy to God. But what else had I done? I had been told before that, though my father is ill, he is staying on this planet until I am stronger. I had just proven that I am stronger in so many ways, on so many levels. What had I done?

Then I knew. I knew why Uncle Jim had come. He wanted me to know he would help my father, his brother, cross over when it was time to go, just as I had done for him. This brought me great comfort. My parents are still so very much in love. My father will be reluctant to leave my mother behind; they have been married for over fifty years. He also claims he is an atheist, and he may not intuitively go to the light. Now I know my Uncle Jim will be there to help him. Thank you, Uncle. I will be there, too.

= Spirits on the Move =

Many of us have our own ideas about how and when spirits come to visit us. Yet the idea that my dad, who is living, could so clearly be with me when he was also present in his actual physical body 200 kilometers away is more difficult to understand.

Have you ever been driving and realized that you are at your destination but barely remember driving there? It is as if you are on auto pilot. This can also happen when we are in boring meetings or when we are zoned out watching television. One could say we are not fully present in the moment. Part of us, but not all of us, is there. Our highest self, our spirit, has temporarily left our body. We can still function, but we are not fully aware. Our highest self may be visiting a loved one, as my father was visiting me. We are amazing beings, with physical bodies and etheric bodies. When these two bodies briefly separate, we can be in two places at once. Our physical self could be at work, and our spirit could be far away, comforting a loved one or exploring the galaxy. When we do this, it is called astral travel.

We can also do this traveling at night. Sylvia Browne estimates that we routinely astral-travel an average of two to three times per week during our sleep (*Phenomenon*, 29). When you have that feeling that you are falling, falling, falling as you drift off to sleep, your spirit is likely leaving your body to astral-travel. Don't worry, you will return to exactly where you are supposed to be. In fact, when you do return, you might find that your body jerks suddenly, waking you up.

My belief in this ability is very strong, partly because I have experienced it in this lifetime and in past lifetimes, but also because it resonates as one of my truths. That is why I believe that people in comas are not trapped in their human bodies; their spirits are free to come and go. I have a vivid past-life memory where I, as a young pregnant woman alongside many of my sisters, was tied to a cross in a meadow.

> I saw myself in a small village of simple homes made of mud and grass. My sisters and I were being chased from our home, as it was being lit on fire by a man on a horse with a torch. We were all dressed the same, in crisp pilgrim-style dresses. My name was Mary and I was about seven months pregnant. My current friends and relatives, Gail, Marci, and Carmen, were my pilgrim sisters. We sisters, along with many other women, were tied to crosses and lined up in orderly fashion in a huge meadow with mountains in the distance. The grassy meadow was filled with women on crosses, persecuted for being witches. Our homes burned in the distance and the fire was sweeping its way across the grassy meadow. I clearly saw myself with child, in the back row of all the rows of women on crosses. I calmly accepted that the fire would reach

us soon, but I was sad that our persecutors did not know any better. I prayed, and convinced everyone to leave their bodies before they were ravaged by the fire. I watched peacefully as the energy flowed out the top of everyone's head in a wavy pattern, leaving the earthly meadow, and man's destruction, behind.

This wonderful ability we have to travel through space and time is truly a gift. I hope that this ability brings you much comfort and joy. I invite you to be aware when your highest self has left your body. Many circumstances require that you return to your body by breathing your higher self in and grounding so that you are fully present in the moment. There are other times when you may want to be fully aware of, and engaged in, the astral travel. There are references to astral travel in a variety of books, so please explore further if you are curious. A brief yet wonderful introduction to this concept can be found in Sylvia Browne's *Phenomenon*. Happy trails to you!

7. Dolphins

═ My Dolphin Odyssey ═

As my husband, Craig, and I left our home on the Canadian prairies to travel to one of the Hawaiian islands for the dolphin retreat, I had no idea what would awaken within me. In this moment I hesitate to record this odyssey on paper, as I am not sure I can convey the depth of what I experienced. The simplicity of the events defies the magnitude of the joy I felt. The joy was seemingly endless, day after day.

I suppose I first noticed my profound connection to the sea when Craig and I arrived at the beautiful house on the bay where our retreat was to take place. As we stood overlooking the bay, I told him that I had a sense that Greece either looked or felt like this. I mentioned it three or four times to him, then consciously chose to stop talking about it because even I thought it was a weird observation. I have yet to visit Greece in this lifetime. Besides, what did Greece have to do with Hawaii? Several days passed before I understood the connection.

In the meantime, we began snorkeling in our bay and in nearby bays in hopes of finding ourselves among a pod of dolphins. Hannelore's Communing with Dolphins retreats are known around the world for the opportunities they provide to interact in meaningful and gentle ways with playful dolphins and other sea life. Hannelore and her island assistants instill within retreat participants respect and love for the dolphins, whales, and all of sea life. Indeed, all that the magnificent island has to offer was to be respected and honored. And it was.

The first day I snorkeled I discovered coral, brightly colored tropical fish, and a magnificent turtle. After swimming that morning I sat in the warm black sand and buried my body in it, like a child. I felt fabulous! I felt grounded and connected to Mother Earth, so very blessed. On the way back we discovered a treasured monk seal resting comfortably on a lava rock beach. This sighting too was a blessing because monk seals are on the endangered species list. Back at our own bay we saw whales spouting and dolphins swimming over the next few days. It truly was paradise.

Honestly, I had so many profound encounters with the dolphins that the memories are already running together. However, I remember clearly the first time I swam with them. I heard them before I saw them. Then there they were, swimming past me and under me. I expected to be frightened the first time I encountered them, but I was not. I hung quietly under the surface of the water. Telepathically, I thanked them for coming and told them I loved them. I also told them I was listening. Then I put my right hand on my heart and listened with my heart. The next thing I knew I experienced an unbelievably beautiful state of bliss: a sense of calm, a sense of serenity, a sense of joy like none other I have ever experienced. I hung in that stillness, that joy, that peace. The message I heard in my heart was not one of words or symbols; it was one of pure love.

I also clearly remember the love in the air the evening we set out on Captain Mike's boat. Later we would discover love was in the water, too. I sat on the bow of the boat with my legs dangling over the edge, enjoying the wind and ocean spray, rocking with the movement of the sea. Two of our guides, Dolphin Dave and Forest, were drumming and playing the didgeridoo directly behind me. I could feel the heartbeat of Mother Earth within me. The sun was setting in a breathtaking display of colors. My senses were heightened. I felt one with the energies of the sea . . . of the entire planet. Amid the joy that we felt, the dolphins appeared. I laughed, I cried as the dolphins playfully swam around our boat.

They were spinner dolphins. They jumped into the air and spun themselves around gloriously. I could clearly see them as they swam under the boat, under my feet, and jumped into the waves ahead. Just to the left of the boat, eight dolphins dove into the same wave at the same time. It was spectacular! There must have been twenty dolphins freely expressing their beauty, their joy, and their love. As the sun set, I began to recognize swelling within me, my own profound connection to the dolphins and to the sea.

The retreat continued. I experienced deep learning in and out of the sea. One afternoon I met with Susan at the beach on our bay. Susan channels messages from the dolphins and whales. As my session with her unfolded, it became apparent she has much to offer. It was Susan who told me that in a past life in a bay (much like our bay), on the island of Crete in Greece, I swam with dolphins daily, sometimes even riding on their backs through the water. Aha! I then understood why I associated being in our bay with Greece. She told me about the beings of light who surround me and support me in my journey. I knew of them and have called upon them often. Susan felt, as I do, that I am on the right path. She told me about my gifts and who I really am. I became increasingly uncomfortable as she talked. She sensed this and reassured me this was not about ego, not about being more or less of who I am. She told me that she has a sense that I am one who takes on the pain of others, specifically of Mother Earth and of women. I had recently come to understand this and I nodded my head, barely holding back my tears. This confirmation was helpful. Susan then shared that she was concerned that I felt I wasn't worthy of these gifts. I burst into tears. That is exactly how I felt. She tenderly explained that I am worthy. I really wanted to believe her.

Susan invited me out from under the majestic tree where we were talking on the edge of the beach, onto the lava rock beach to clear away the layers that made me feel unworthy. I planted my feet solidly on two rocks, opened up my arms palms up, and closed my eyes. I began to speak softly, releasing fear, pain, and feelings of unworthiness to Mother Earth, to the whales, and to the dolphins.

Within minutes Susan began shouting to me in excitement that the dolphins had come to help. I opened my eyes, and there they were in the water, right in front of me, much closer than even seemed possible. Susan directed me into the water. Thankfully, I had my swimsuit on, so I threw off my sarong. It did not matter that I had no goggles, no snorkel, nor any fins; under Susan's watchful eye I swam a few feet.

The dolphins were near, as was a whale farther out in the bay. I began releasing all sorts of dense, heavy pain. In a voice building like a crescendo in a powerful symphony, I thanked the sea for washing away lifetimes of pain and suffering on behalf of women everywhere. I thanked the Universe for bringing unconditional love into the lives of women and their children. I thanked Spirit for helping women everywhere to be whole . . . and, when the time was right, for them to find a love like the love my husband and I share, in whatever form that may be. I thanked God for helping mothers and fathers on this planet, in this galaxy, to truly love their children, no matter what. I thanked the Universe for helping women, men, and children everywhere to open up to the love that surrounds them. I thanked Mother Earth for her beauty and abundance. I told her how sorry I am that we do not always honor her, that we hurt her, abuse her. I thanked the sky, land, and sea animals for their beauty and wisdom. I thanked the dolphins and whales for their part in healing our planet. I bellowed these thanks from deep within me. *I felt it. I knew it.*

I know the dolphins did too, for they swam in circles around Susan and me. They swam round and round and round as I declared my gratitude. *I felt it, really felt it.* My prayer was complete.

Susan was delighted that the dolphins had come to help and be present in such a meaningful, visible manner. She felt the dolphins and whales would take the message around the world and that people everywhere would benefit. I felt I had been baptized and was, if only briefly, truly one with All That Is. As directed by Susan, I returned to the shore, where I sat on a throne, which is ever present in the lava rock. I gave thanks and grounded the healing fully into my physical body.

= Swimming with Dolphins =

Interestingly, tales of such experiences between humans and dolphins have been common throughout history: "One of the earliest confirmed representations of dolphins was created by the ancient Minoans on the island of Crete in 3500 BCE" (Dudzinki and Frohoff, 2008, 117). By the time Aristotle labeled cetaceans, including dolphins and whales, as mammals in his *History of Animals*, Greek fishermen already spoke of their special bond with humans (Wurtz, 2003, 8). Indeed, there is evidence of myths and legends about the affinity between dolphins, whales, and humans in petroglyphs dating back 9,000 years (Dudzinki and Frohoff, 117). "According to the Bible, the first animal God created was the whale" (Wurtz, 12).

After many years of work in the 1950s and 1960s, researcher John Lilly came to believe that dolphins are an extraterrestrial intelligence, equal in intelligence to humans (Dudzinki and Frohoff, 119). This belief and Lilly's prophecies were, and continue to be, controversial among academics.

Coastal peoples have many legends to share, with strikingly similar details and themes (Wurtz, 8). Some of the legends appear to be mythical, when in fact they are true. For instance, a killer whale named Old Tom helped whalers in Twofold Bay for approximately twenty years sometime between 1860 and his death of old age in 1930. Old Tom reportedly went so far as to drag the whalers' catch to shore as he helped the fishermen (Wurtz, 12).

Dolphins reportedly help others who are in danger. These behaviors have been observed in the wild. Not only will mothers carry their dead calves on the surface in an attempt to help them breathe, dolphins will help fellow dolphins having difficulty swimming (Wurtz, 68). Dolphins have also been known to help humans. Some might argue that they do so because they see us as one of them. I believe that their desire to assist us is related more to the affinity that we share than to our physiological similarities.

For me, being in the presence of dolphins and whales felt like being totally present; my highest self and my body were one, and I was one with the dolphins, the sea, the planet, and All That Is. Ackerman (2003), as quoted by Curtin and Wilkes (*Swimming with Captive Dolphins*, 2007), states that swimming with dolphins "obscures the division between animal and human and provides an imaginary 'at-one-ment' with nature." It was definitely an at-one-moment for me. Was it also atonement? It was not for me in a traditional sense, as I don't believe in labelling our transgressions as sins; rather, I see them as lessons. I believe God is all-loving and nonjudgmental. This experience, however, left me feeling more forgiving toward myself and others. I needed to be in this place of forgiveness in order to get past my feelings of unworthiness of my gifts identified by Susan.

This was reinforced during my session with Susan. I shared with her that I noticed other swimmers (not of our group) thrashing about in an attempt to be near the dolphins and take their pictures. I knew in my heart that all I needed to do to be near the dolphins was to be still and be present in the moment. My overall experience was so blissful I was only mildly annoyed with the other swimmers. Through Susan the dolphins told me to forgive the other swimmers because they didn't know any better. My friend and teacher Hannelore tells us that when people know better, they do better. I believe that. I know that we, as those who love dolphins, can do better.

There is no doubt in my heart that dolphins like to be with humans under certain circumstances. Dudzinki and Frohoff clearly state, "It is not unusual for dolphins to initiate social contact with humans," and "Dolphins typically are extremely interested in humans" (117,133). Many others, including some of my dear friends, describe playful, joyful interactions between humans and dolphins. And yet the United States Marine Mammal Protection Act of 1972 (amended in 1994) was deemed necessary in order to protect our precious whales, dolphins, and other marine mammals. This act prohibits human interactions with certain marine mammals that may change their behavior, harass them, or cause their death. Some researchers argue that swimming with dolphins does result in change of behavior; therefore, swimming with dolphins in the wild in the United States is to be considered illegal. Obviously not everyone agrees. I believe quality swim-with-dolphin programs can operate without harassing or harming free-ranging dolphins.

Dolphins in captivity live under a variety of conditions, ranging from seemingly acceptable to totally inadequate. At my current level of understanding of the issues, I choose not to swim with dolphins in captivity. I can't possibly support confining such intelligent and spiritual beings to life in captivity away from their families and their natural environment.

I have awakened to my love of the sea, dolphins, and whales. I am very, very grateful. I have no idea where this new understanding will take me next. I am honored to share this story with you, and yet I am compelled to help you make ethical and loving decisions about interacting with dolphins and whales. If you choose to swim with dolphins, I suggest that you visit Hannelore's Web site www.communingwithdolphins. com and read *The Official Dolphin Swim Guide*. Please educate yourself about issues related to interacting with dolphins. Research the organization providing your experience.

I believe dolphins and whales have a great deal to teach us. You do not need to be near them to learn from them. You can listen to their channeled messages in Hannelore's CD *Communing with Dolphins.* You can read about them in *Dolphin Mysteries* (Dudzinki and Frohoff) or *Dolphins and Whales* (Wurtz). You can see them through Dolphin Dave's eyes in David Jimenez's profoundly beautiful and insightful art available through his Web site www.dolphindave.com You can explore your connection to dolphins, even over the phone, with Susan by contacting her at sperepelken@hotmail.com You can know them in your own heart, in your own way.

8. Making Your Dreams Take Flight

= A Mother's Wish =

As I fled the public washroom in the airport, a proper lady scolded me in her southern drawl, "Pardon ME!" I thought to myself, "She sure is rude. What's HER problem?" Then, even in my haste, I realized I had been the rude one. I had come bursting out of a toilet stall, throwing my backpack over my shoulder, with my head down, determined to board my connecting flight to Calgary. I was so focused on my goal that I almost ran into her. As I rushed by I mumbled, "Sorry."

I ran, with my husband in tow, from one end of the airport to the other to catch that flight home. My husband had been content to stand patiently in line with hundreds of other people to get information about our connecting flight. I was not!

I knew in my heart we could make the flight. I had willed it to be so as we sat in our last plane waiting on the tarmac. We had waited several hours for a rainstorm to clear. Then our flight was further delayed as we waited for our turn on the runway in New Orleans. Added to this was another delay as we waited for our turn to land in Houston. It was important for me to be home that day. My husband didn't understand how much it meant to me. He was impatient with the intensity of my emotions when we were told we had likely missed our connecting flight because our plane was so very late. I knew we could make it, and it angered me that he was willing to wait around for more information. That's when I told him I was going to make a run for the gate, whether he joined me or not. He stepped over turnstiles and off we went. I was fuelled by anger and hope.

Out of breath, we arrived at the gate. I was devastated when I saw that the area was empty and the plane was loaded, perhaps even gone. I spoke politely but urgently with the airline staff. Yes, the plane was loaded; the doors were closed and the plane was about to depart. Yet they kindly delayed their departure and opened the doors, allowing us to board. As we boarded, we discovered that our seats had been reassigned to someone else and we were going to be separated. A generous person offered to move so we could sit together. This was truly a blessing because we were delayed another two hours on the runway before our plane was cleared for final takeoff. After we landed in Calgary and cleared customs, it was obvious we were going to be late for our dinner in Red Deer, which was still a ninety-minute drive away, so we called our guests and changed the reservation by one hour. I was elated!

Our journey had started at 5:00 a.m., when we left the hotel in New Orleans; we reached Red Deer at 6:50 p.m. Oh, what a ride. It should only have been a four-and-a-half-hour flight. Miraculously, our luggage made it as well. I don't know how.

At 6:50 p.m. we walked into the restaurant. My heart was pounding with gratitude and excitement. I immediately went to the washroom to freshen up.

Then, with a smile as big as my heart, I greeted our son, Aaron, and his friends as they arrived. I was so grateful to be there. I had to be home to celebrate his eighteenth birthday. His father, my husband, didn't think it was that big a deal if we didn't make it back on time, as long as we had tried. I was initially even hesitant to go to the conference in New Orleans, but we were able to plan it so that we could be home on Aaron's eighteenth birthday. After all, we should have had plenty of time. With support from the Universe I created the happy ending to this story.

Why was it so important to me to be there on Aaron's birthday, when we had an entire weekend to celebrate with friends and family? To understand this, you need to understand how intensely I love my children. You also need to understand that I have always held myself to impossibly high standards as a mother; partly because I had wanted so desperately to be a mother since I was a child myself, and because my children's birth parents wanted more for their babies than they could give them at the time. Out of love, respect, and recognition of their extreme sacrifice, our children will always have more. Not more things! But more of their father and me; more of us. Another reason this day was so important to me is that Aaron seems to have been waiting to be an adult all of this lifetime. I believe that this may be the very first lifetime he was not living the life of an adult by the time he was twelve or thirteen years old. I believe reaching "adulthood" as defined by our society was a huge milestone for him. I knew I had to be there for him, and with him. And I was.

== Creating What You Desire ==

How did I create this, or how did I will this to occur? You may ask, "Who are you, Deb Suchy, to believe that you have so much power?" I am a child of the Universe. I am part of God, just as all things are. Spirit is within me. The law of attraction tells us that we get more of what we focus on. I chose not to focus on my frustration or anger in this situation, although I did allow myself to feel that and let it go. Instead I focussed on being home for Aaron's birthday dinner and how wonderful that was going to *feel*. It is my understanding that placing your attention on a goal is not nearly as powerful as focussing on the feelings related to the achievement of the goal. So as we sat in the plane on the runway, I closed my eyes and imagined the plane taking off, and how great that was going to feel. I imagined going through the motions of checking my seatbelt, returning my seat to an upright position, and latching the tray in front of me. In my mind's eye I saw the landscape roll by. I re-created that cool sensation I get in my chest every time I feel a plane leave the runway. In my own mind I gave thanks that I was on my way and that I would be there in time for my son's eighteenth birthday. I felt the anticipation, the excitement, and the gratitude. In my mind's eye and in my heart, I was already there.

As I put out to the Universe that my husband and I would arrive in time for our son's eighteenth birthday dinner, I also asked and trusted that all taking place was taking place for the highest good for all. I understood that no matter how passionately I wished for this to happen, the Divine, including my higher, sometimes unconscious self, may have other plans for me or my son. I released my attachment to my hope to be home in time. Then I trusted.

Gregg Braden labels this practice the lost mode of prayer in his book *Secrets of the Lost Mode of Prayer* (2006). Lynn Grabhorn talks about this strategy in *Excuse Me: Your Life is Waiting* (2000). Still others would label this strategy "The Secret," as described by Rhonda Byrne in her book of the same name (2006).

Was I able to stay in that place of trust throughout our very long day? Nope. I had a couple of private hissy fits along the way, but they were brief. I always returned my focus to being there with my son. And, I didn't sit and wait for it to all unfold.

- I set my intention.

- I imagined how grateful I felt, as if I were already there.

- Then I took action.

I ran to the other end of that airport. I spoke up at the gate. I didn't wait for Spirit to make things happen. Spirit works through me . . . in me . . . IS me (and you). I believe that when I take action from my heart, intending that my action be for the highest good of all concerned, Spirit is present and supportive. That is God helping me. Thank you, God.

I encourage you to explore the law of attraction and learn how to create what your heart truly desires. In fact, this topic may very well be your starting point in your own journey. I read Lynn Grabhorn's book first, then Gregg Braden's, followed by Rhonda Byrne's. Reading them in this order was perfect for me. You will need to find what works best for you.

= Conclusion =

It truly has been an honor to share my journey thus far with you. Alignment with moose medicine has served me well in the telling of my story. As I shared in my introduction: I suggest that you read many different books, study with many different teachers, and surround yourself with others who are on this journey. I wish you many, many blessings as you find your own way back to who you really are. As my understanding is ever-evolving and shifting, I invite you to stay tuned to my journey through offerings on my Web site, www.joyfulcreating.ca. If you are interested in learning more about grounding yourself deeply and safely in Mother Earth, please watch for my *Ribbons of Light* CD on my Web site. Also watch for my next book, *Jimmy the Grounding Tree*. It is a beautifully illustrated "children's book," written for children and adults. Namaste, dear friend . . .

$=$ Recommended Reading $=$

Andrews, Ted. *Animal Speak: The Spiritual and Magical Powers of Creatures Great and Small.* Woodbury, MN: Llewellyn Publications, 1993.

Braden, Gregg. *Secrets of the Lost Mode of Prayer.* Carlsbad, CA: Hay House, Inc., 2006.

Browne, Sylvia. *Phenomenon: Everything You Need to Know About the Paranormal.* New York: Penguin Group, 2005.

Browne, Sylvia, and Lindsay Harrison. *Past Lives, Future Healing.* New York: New American Library, 2001.

Byrne, Rhonda. *The Secret.* Hillsboro, OR: TS Production Limited Liability Company/Atria Books/Beyond Words Publishing, 2006.

Curtin, S. C., and K. Wilkes. "Swimming with Captive Dolphins: Current Debates and Post-Experience Dissonance." *International Journal of Tourism Research* 9. no. 2 (2007): 131–146. Bournemouth, UK, Bournemouth University Research Online (BURO).

Dudzinki, Kathleen M., and Tony Frohoff, Tony. *Dolphin Mysteries: Unlocking Secrets of Communication*. New Haven, CT: Yale University Press, 2008.

Farmer, Steven D. *Animal Spirit Guides*. Carlsbad, CA: Hay House, Inc., 2006.

Grabhorn, Lynn. *Excuse Me, Your Life Is Waiting: The Astonishing Power of Feelings*. Charlottesville, VA: Hampton Roads Publishing Company, Inc., 2000.

Hall, Judy. *The Illustrated Guide to Crystals*. New York: Godsfield Press, 2000.

Hay, Louise L. *You Can Heal Your Life*. Carlsbad, CA: Hay House, Inc., 1987.

Linn, Denise. *Past Lives, Present Miracles*. Carlsbad, CA: Hay House, Inc., 2008.

Melody. *Love Is in the Earth: A Kaleidoscope of Crystals.* Wheat Ridge, CO: Earth-Love Publishing House, 1995.

Sams, Jamie, and D. Carson. *Medicine Cards: The Discovery of Power Through the Ways of the Animals.* New York: St. Martin's Press, 1999.

Stein, Diane. *Essential Reiki: A Complete Guide to an Ancient Healing Art.* Berkeley, CA: The Crossing Press, 1995.

Tolle, Eckhart. *A New Earth: Awakening to Your Life's Purpose.* New York: Plume/Penguin Group, 2005.

Virtue, Doreen. *Earth Angels.* Carlsbad, CA: Hay House, Inc., 2002.

Williamson, Marianne. *A Return to Love.* New York: HarperCollins, 1992.

Wurtz, Maurizio, and Nadia Repetto. *Dolphins and Whales.* Edited by Valeria Manferto De Fabianis and Laura Accomazzo. Vercelli, Italy: White Star Publishers, 2003.

= Notes =

= Notes =

....

....

....

....

....

....

....

....

....

....

....

....

....

= Notes =

= Notes =

= Notes =

— Notes —

Notes

Printed in the United States
151872LV00001B/26/P